T0062167

Renown Unique

Tulips

A LITTLE BOOK OF FLOWERS

Tara Austen Weaver

Illustrations by Emily Poole

SASQUATCH BOOKS

SEATTLE

For my mother, whose garden was full
of the reddest tulips. As a child, I didn't
know red tulips symbolized the deepest,
most abiding sort of love, but even then,
I could feel it.

Long live the tulip! This brightly colored jewel brightens our days in early spring. We truly look forward to seeing those blue-green leaves start to emerge as the Earth awakens from its winter sleep!

—CATHERINE BOECKMANN

Apricot Beauty

Contents

Origin of the Species

The tulip is a flower that draws some of the most exquisite lines in nature and then, in spasms of extravagance, blithely oversteps them.

—MICHAEL POLLAN

Alba Coerulea Oculata

Little Beauty

"Tulips were a tray of jewels," wrote E. M. Forster in his novel *Howards End*, and the gem comparison is an apt one. After a drab winter, tulips sally forth with their long stems and oval-shaped buds opening to blooms all colors of the rainbow—from deep scarlet and purple, to the Easter egg pastels of pink, lavender, and pale yellow. Tulips come striped, painted in contrasting colors, or rimmed in white or gold. Swaying, as they do, above the new growth of a spring garden, tulips are a symbol of rebirth, as colorful and triumphant as a flower could be.

The story of tulips weaves through political and economic history like few other flowers. These humble bulbs we tuck into garden beds have been gifted by sultans and queens; they have been celebrated, stolen, carried across oceans and plains; and at times they have been considered as precious as rubies. Happily for us, these days they are an affordable luxury—and easy to grow as well. More than anything else, tulips are a gift we give ourselves. The bulbs we plant each year are an act of hope that has played out for centuries—the hope that this small autumnal effort will yield great beauty come spring.

Modern-day tulips trace their roots to a swath of territory stretching from the Mediterranean across Central Asia and up into the Tian Shan mountain range. Tulips have been able to thrive in climates with cold winters and hot, dry summers, as their bulbs allow the plant to go dormant and store energy for the next spring. While the wild species are shorter and smaller than our modern-day hybrids, they share the same six petals and elongated gray-green foliage recognized throughout the world.

The earliest known physical record of tulips dates to illustrations in a twelfth-century bible, where the text is embellished with images of the flowers. Tulips were certainly cultivated before that time, but the history has been lost. Mention of the flowers do show up in several versions of ancient legend, however. In one, a Persian youth is so heartbroken over the loss of his beloved that he mounts a favorite horse and rides it at full speed off the edge of a cliff to his death. It is said that red tulips sprouted from the ground that was soaked in his blood. Another story tells of a lovelorn young man rejected by his sweetheart, who cries with the pain of heartbreak. Where his tears fall to the ground, tulips grow. For generations now, tulips have been a symbol of great love.

Tulips also feature in early Persian poetry, written during the Islamic Golden Age (eighth to thirteenth centuries). "In the flaming light of the morning sky," wrote Omar Khayyam (1048–1131), a scholar, mathematician, astronomer, philosopher, and poet, "the wine in your cup looks like a tulip in spring." Another poem, by the theologian, Islamic scholar, and Sufi mystic Jalāl al-Dīn Muhammad Rūmī (1207–1273)—more commonly known today as Rumi—also refers to the flowers:

"December and January, gone.
Tulips coming up."

It was in sixteenth-century Turkey, however, and the Ottoman court of Suleiman I that tulips rose to royal prominence. Suleiman I (1494–1566) was a powerful ruler whose interests extended from politics to poetry and plants, and he made tulips the official flower of his court. The English name *tulip* is said to come from Westerners adopting the Turkish word for turban, which the flowers were thought to resemble. Men also sometime wore tulips tucked in their turbans as decoration. In Turkey, however, tulips are referred to by their Persian name: lale (pronounced "lah-lay"). Because the word uses the same Arabic letters as Allah, tulips were considered flowers of God.

The Turkish passion for tulips continued long after Suleiman's reign. Lâle Devri—the Tulip Age—took place under Sultan Ahmed III, who ruled in the early 1700s. Tom Lodewijk, in *The Book of Tulips*, describes the annual tulip festival held during this period. "Hundreds of exquisite vases were filled with the most expensive tulips available and were placed on stands decorated with crystal balls filled with colored water. Crystal lanterns cast an enchanting glow throughout the gardens. Canaries and nightingales in cages hung on branches to delight the guests with their song." Apparently the guests were required to wear colors that harmonized with the flowers. Tulips became a symbol of the Ottoman Empire, seen in decorative paintings from that period on ceramic and tile.

It was from Istanbul (then called Constantinople), a city that often served as a gateway between the East and the West, that tulips were first introduced to Europe. The details of exactly how and when have not been recorded, but one of the few references we have comes from a Swiss botanist by the name of Conrad Gessner (1516–1565), who wrote of seeing a deep-red tulip in 1559, in Augsburg (present-day Germany). It was in a garden that belonged to Johannis

Heinrich Herwart, a magistrate. The tulip, he said, had been grown from seed brought from Constantinople. Gessner described the flower in great detail, later illustrating it in a full-color woodcut.

Tulips came to the Netherlands in part through the work of Carolus Clusius, who became head botanist at the University of Leiden in 1593. Born in present-day France, Clusius was well connected in the plant world and frequently received seeds and bulbs from far-off places. He established the imperial botanical garden in Vienna at the invitation of the Holy Roman Emperor Maximilian II, and he was friends with the Austrian ambassador to the Ottoman Empire, so it is likely the bulbs came through one of those channels. Clusius planted tulips when he first arrived in Leiden, and when they bloomed he received numerous offers to buy the bulbs—but he refused to sell them. The flowers must have made quite an impression because would-be buyers crept into the garden in the dark of night and stole the tulip bulbs.

Interest in tulips spread in Western Europe as bulbs were traded and sold by travelers, merchants, and botanists—as well as by artists, who were especially taken with these unique, long-stemmed blooms. Tulips were bred far beyond their original wild forms into more dramatic cultivars. Both the ease of trading bulbs and a growing merchant class that enjoyed the modest luxury of flowers meant that tulips found an eager and appreciative audience. But nowhere did they make more of an impact than in the newly formed northern coastal country of the Netherlands.

At this time, the Netherlands was the wealthiest country in Europe. Their vast trading empire was based on shipping—started when the Dutch began transporting wheat from the Baltic countries. The Netherlands soon grew to challenge the might of the Portuguese and Spanish maritime trade, eventually setting up a colonial empire with outposts around the globe, from the tip of Africa to the Hudson River Valley, the Caribbean, South America, and throughout Asia—particularly the islands now known as Indonesia. Unlike other colonial powers that claimed land, the Dutch focused on trade—sugar, spices, tobacco, chocolate, gold, ivory, and the transportation and sale of enslaved people. The Dutch merchant fleets also engaged in piracy, attacking and plundering Spanish and Portuguese ships.

Dutch trade was conducted by two private merchant companies that functioned like foreign arms of the Dutch government—seizing valuable assets and territory in other countries. The Dutch West India Company traded in Africa, the Caribbean, and the Americas, while the Dutch United East India Company (known as the VOC) operated in Asia. The VOC was the first multinational corporation financed by shares—funded by the government but also by private investors—and the Dutch established the first stock exchange. This put the idea of investment in future shares—a piece of paper that represented goods—into the public consciousness.

At the same time that Dutch fortunes were being made, tulips were becoming more desirable—with unique shapes and colors being bred each year. Most popular were the "Broken" tulips, which featured petals streaked with flames of irregular color: red on white background, gold on scarlet. These streaks are caused by a virus passed along by aphid infestations, but at the time the effect seemed random and uncontrolled; this made the bulbs even more valuable and sought after.

The Dutch had recently won their independence from the Spanish Hapsburgs, and after years of chafing under the rule of a Catholic monarchy, many in the Netherlands were embracing Protestantism. Dutch Protestant values promoted hard work and modesty, and looked down on ostentatious displays of wealth, which smacked of their former Spanish overlords. Protestants also rejected depictions of religious icons—no paintings of the holy family, no bible scenes—as it was thought to cheapen them. Instead, increasingly well-to-do merchant families in Europe's wealthiest country commissioned paintings to decorate their new and now larger homes—portraits, still life paintings, and more. And to show their prosperity in an understated way, they posed with tulips. Decorative gardens had always been a sign of wealth; now these expensive blooms were a status symbol as well.

In the 1630s, this fascination with tulips resulted in what many consider the first economic bubble—called *Tulpenwoede* in Dutch (tulip mania). Because of the nature of the flowers, those who invested in tulips were buying bulbs that had not yet been harvested—future shares, as it were. These trades did not take place on a regulated exchange, but in the rooms of local pubs and saloons, and prices were whatever someone would pay. At one point, a single bulb of the most coveted cultivar—the red and white flamed tulip 'Semper Augustus'—sold for 10,000 guilders,

A VISUAL LANGUAGE

Because the Dutch Reformed Church explicitly forbade the use of religious iconography, artists of the seventeenth century found ways to disguise their messages by developing a secret language of symbols. This shows up most significantly in the many still life paintings that survive from this period. What might look like the remains of a meal to the average viewer today actually held a coded message—bread symbolized the body of Christ, oysters warn against temptation, and meat or shellfish speak to the corrupting influence of wealth and gluttony. Dragonflies are signs of the devil, butterflies symbolize salvation, and snails—which are able to reproduce asexually—signify the Virgin Mary.

When it came to floral still life paintings, the code of symbolism was included in the book *Het Groot Schilderboek*, based on lectures by the artist Gérard de Lairesse (1641–1711). While paintings of expensive, cultivated flowers spoke generally to wealth and prosperity, each flower had its own significance—a forerunner to the language of flowers popular in the Victorian era. In Dutch still life paintings, violets symbolize modesty, carnations refer to eternal life, ivy signifies the resurrection, while sheaves of wheat are a sign of Christ. And the tulip, which features so prominently in floral still life paintings of the era, symbolizes nobility. Knowing this, it's easy to understand why aspiring and newly wealthy Dutch merchants were so eager to align themselves with these beguiling flowers.

about the same price as a house in the most desirable area of Amsterdam at that time. Such speculation was unsustainable, and the Dutch tulip bubble collapsed in 1637, leaving investors and aspiring tulip fanciers with sheaves of paper now worthless.

The Netherlands was not the only country to have embraced the tulip. A version of the Dutch tulip mania took place in France between 1634 and 1639, with aristocratic women wearing tulips on the neckline of their gowns like jewels. A single bulb of a red-and-white-striped tulip was used in place of a wedding dowry. Bred by the bride's father, the tulip was named, appropriately enough, 'Mariage de ma Fille' (marriage of my daughter). As Anna Pavord writes in her seminal book on the flower, tulips were "the most sought-after, costly, and prestigious flowers that a seventeenth-century gardener could possess."

Tulips crossed the English Channel at some point in the middle of the 1500s, likely brought by Flemish settlers, who had been breeding tulips for some time. Flanders is also credited with introducing tulips to the French. By the early 1600s, tulips were well established in English gardens—adopted by the wealthy as a symbol of prestige and planted on the grounds of castles and grand estates. It became fashionable to plant arrangements of bulbs on parterres and in formal knots, and wealthy aristocrats submitted orders for tulip bulbs by the hundreds—and occasionally thousands. Tulip breeding was also taken up as a hobby by craftsmen in England on a smaller, more deliberate scale, where it continues on to this day (see page 113).

Tulips made their way to the colonies of North America via Dutch traders and settlers, who controlled areas of present-day New York, New Jersey, Connecticut, and Delaware in the early 1600s. They were carried by those who wanted a small but significant reminder of home. The Puritan settler group who arrived on the *Mayflower* in 1620 had lived in Leiden before their journey, though we know of no connection to the tulip trade.

Tulip bulbs once drove the Dutch to a spending frenzy, but they also have provided a pillar for their economy. Flower bulbs thrive in the low-lying sandy soil of the Netherlands, near the sea, where the rain and cold winters help with bulb formation. The Netherlands now produces 80 percent of all flower bulbs grown worldwide, not just tulips, and the Royal FloraHolland flower auction in Aalsmeer is the largest in the world. In 2020, the Netherlands tulip bulb trade brought in more than 220 million euros, with additional money to be made in the cut flower market; the Dutch devotion to the tulip has been well repaid.

How amazing, really, that these humble bulbs have traveled the world—carried along the Central Asian trading routes, exchanged for riches, tucked into pockets, mailed to foreign countries, even consumed in times of strife. It's the unique nature of the tulip that makes it possible—a bulb that goes dormant for months at a time, yet springs into life with water and warmth. How lucky we are to have tulips: so much beauty from the most unassuming little package.

THE HUNGER WINTER

Tulips have played an integral role in Dutch history—but never as much as the winter of 1944–1945, during World War II, when Nazi forces blockaded supply routes as a way to punish the Dutch for their resistance. The resulting famine affected some 4.5 million people; it is estimated as many as 22,000 people starved.

This period is called the Hunger Winter—*Hongerwinter*. As food stores ran out, the Dutch turned to the prior year's harvest of tulip bulbs. These bulbs were old and dry, but people were desperate. They ate tulips—and the sugar beets that were normally fed to livestock—and they burned furniture to cook and stay warm.

The Dutch Office of Food Supply published a booklet on how to consume tulips, explaining that the brown bulb jacket and the bitter yellow core in the center, which is poisonous, should be removed, but the white layers—called scales—could be eaten. There were recipes for tulip soup and tulip bread. Father Leo Zonneveld, a young boy during the Hunger Winter, said later that the bread tasted like "wet sawdust."

Hongerwinter came to an end with a shipment of flour that was allowed in from Sweden, and the liberation of western Holland by the Allied forces in May of 1945.

Tulip mania wasn't irrational. Tulips were a newish luxury product in a country rapidly expanding its wealth and trade networks. Many more people could afford luxuries—and tulips were seen as beautiful, exotic, and redolent of the good taste and learning displayed by well-educated members of the merchant class.

—ANNE GOLDGAR

Forms of the Flower

We can always recognize a
tulip, even though they can
be so different, like a lion
from a tiger. No other flower
is quite so deeply coded in
our awareness.

—POLLY NICHOLSON

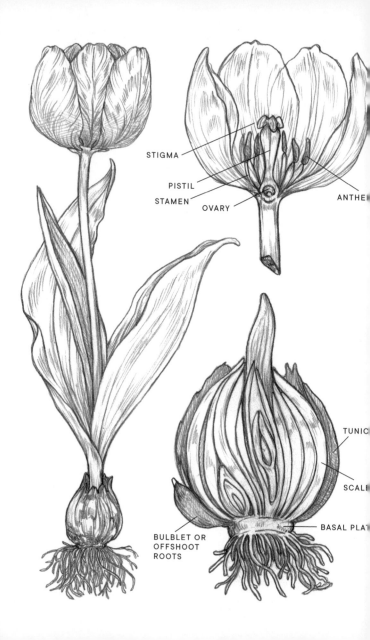

STIGMA

PISTIL

STAMEN

OVARY

ANTHE

TUNIC

SCALI

BASAL PLAT

BULBLET OR
OFFSHOOT
ROOTS

Tulip Botany

Tulips belong to the Liliaceae family—along with other members like lilies and onions. A significant feature is a bulb made up of scales: fleshy layers that are attached at the basal plate, from which roots grow down and a flower stalk ascends. These scales store energy that can be called on to fuel the growth of the plant. Like an onion, each bulb is protected by a tunic of brown, papery skin.

Most tulip bulbs produce a single stem bearing one flower, though there are some multiheaded cultivars. The foliage is quite simple—gray-green elongated leaves, though a few tulip cultivars feature reddish markings on their leaves or a narrow white border along the leaf edge.

Tulip bulbs are planted in late autumn. They lie dormant until conditions trigger their growth. A tulip is a true bulb, in effect a large flower bud. The bud begins to mature over the winter and—in the warmth and extended daylight of spring—will emerge from the soil and bloom. This process causes the mother bulb to produce new side buds that will grow and mature into their own bulbs, though it may take a few years for those new bulbs to produce a flower.

The structure of the tulip is rather simple. The six petals are referred to as tepals (the inner three are technically petals; the outer three are sepals), and they surround a stigma, ovary, and anthers. When a tulip is pollinated and matures, it can produce hundreds of seeds—though it will take up to 7 years for those seeds to produce a flower. The vast majority of tulips are grown by bulb.

KAUFMANNIANA

FOSTERIANA

DARWIN HYBRID

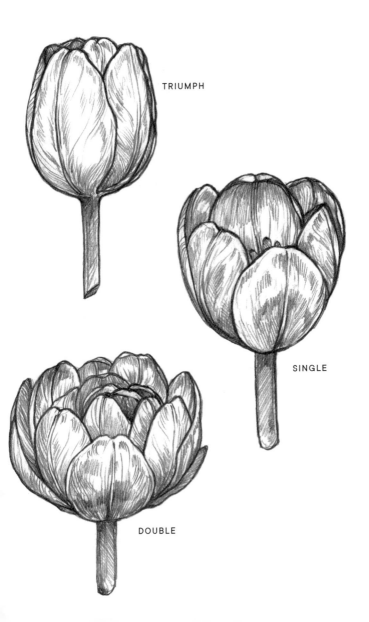

TRIUMPH

SINGLE

DOUBLE

PARROT

FRINGED

GREIGII

LILY-FLOWERED

SPECIES AND
MULTIFLOWERED

Over the years, and with intentional breeding, a wide variety of tulip forms have been developed. There are more than 2,000 tulip cultivars (intentionally cultivated varieties) and approximately 125 wild species tulips. These have been categorized into fifteen groups, based on shape and bloom time. The following is a breakdown of the different groups, along with some recommended cultivars—though there is such wide variety and choice when it comes to tulips, it's impossible to pick favorites. The more one learns about tulips, the easier it is to understand why these bulbs have caused such floral frenzy.

Early Season Tulips

Kaufmanniana

One of the earliest tulips to bloom, the Kaufmanniana group features narrow flowers and pointy-tipped petals—more like a champagne flute than the cupped shape of a wineglass. Found growing wild in Turkistan, they were introduced to Europe in 1877. Kaufmanniana tulips bloom on shorter stems (8 to 10 inches) and are sometimes called waterlily tulips, as the flowers can open quite flat in the sun; they also often feature a spot of contrasting color at the center (this is called a basal blotch). One of the groups that are more likely to perennialize, these short and sturdy flowers get tulip season off to a strong start.

Early Harvest and Giuseppe Verdi

Johann Strauss

'Early Harvest': a vivid apricot color, this tulip has petals that are darker on the outside and often rimmed in gold. Growing only 10 inches, these bronzy-orange blooms feature leaves that are streaked with maroon. With a high likelihood of repeat blooms in years to come, this award-winner adds autumn color to the spring garden.

'Giuseppe Verdi': a flamboyant vision in carmine and yellow, this pointed-petal bloom will open in sunlight until it looks like a gold star. Red streaks on these smaller flowers look bright and cheerful, and are well suited to growing in containers. Likely to perennialize, they are also good for rock gardens and front-of-bed plantings. These bright blooms grow 8 to 10 inches, with light striping on the leaves.

'Heart's Delight': early to flower, this tulip is truly a delight—at 8 to 10 inches, these cheerful blooms bring a combination of pink and red petals with a warm yellow base, white edges, and colored streaks on the leaves. Likely to perennialize, this tulip will be a harbinger of spring for years to come.

'Johann Strauss' ('The First'): this cheerful, sunshine-like bloom has petals streaked in red and white that open to a yellow center. This low grower (6 to 10 inches) looks stunning planted in large drifts. A worthy herald of spring, this tulip is sometimes also called 'The First;' it might just be your first tulip of the season to bloom.

Single Early

Despite its name, Single Early are not the earliest tulips to bloom—they come after the Kaufmanniana group. They feature single, cuplike blooms on shorter stems (10 to 18 inches), and this sturdiness makes them excellent tulips for outdoor containers or bulbs for forcing (planting indoors so the bulbs are "forced" into bloom before they would naturally).

'Apricot Beauty': a well-named favorite, this tulip is a fragrant bit of loveliness, with petals brushed in pale salmon and pink. Looking like spring in flower form, this midseason award-winner grows gracefully on 14- to 16-inch stems. Excellent for forcing and a beautiful cut flower as well (see page 6).

'Pretty Princess': rose pink with flames of orange, darker pink, and sometimes purple, these tulips are a spring dream. The foliage is unique as well, with a narrow band of white on the outer edges that gives a silvery appearance. Sturdy flowers on 12- to 14-inch stems, these will attract attention and brighten up any garden.

'Fire Queen': bringing a splash of color, this tulip produces red-flamed blooms on sturdy stems (12 to 18 inches) that can withstand early spring rains. If you are weary of drab, winter colors, Fire Queen will set your garden alight.

'Flair': blooming in shades of vivid orangey-red rimmed in gold, this tulip is aptly named—a flower that dazzles in sunset colors. Another sturdy tulip, blooming on 10- to 12- inch stems, Flair looks striped when the buds are closed, but opens into a circle of bright yellow around the rim (see page 126).

Pretty Princess

Fire Queen

Tulips are all about levity and rebirth. Their flowers are like ballerinas—they dance.

—SANDRA SIGMAN

Double Early (Peony)

The exuberance of Double Early flowers makes them a firm favorite, with masses of petals perched on sturdy, shorter stems (10 to 12 inches, though some cultivars are taller). Opening into wide flowers, these early to midseason bloomers are lush and appealing. Even those who do not usually fancy tulips may find themselves falling for these multilayered double cultivars.

'Columbus': a vision of raspberry tipped in cream, these blooms are so stuffed with petals, they look far more like a peony than a tulip. These sturdy bloomers (12- to 16-inch stems) are wildly attractive and will liven up a garden bed or a vase with gorgeous layers like a ballerina's skirt.

'Monsella': with rows of brilliant gold and carmine red, this fragrant double bloom will add color to any early spring garden. Monsella tends to produce up to three blooms per bulb, making it a flamboyant fan favorite. A shorter cultivar, with stems only 8 to 12 inches, this tulip will shine on, no matter the weather or the wind.

'Montreux': ivory blooms full of petals and blushed in pale pink or apricot with hints of yellow and possibly green, this tulip has a sweet fragrance and a timeless, romantic look. An excellent cut flower, easy to combine with other blooms in arrangements, Montreux grows 12 to 18 inches on sturdy stems (see page 141).

Columbus

Monsella

Tulips could be considered
the neon lights of the flower
world, for surely their theatrical
colors illuminate otherwise
pale gardens emerging from
winter doldrums.

—BECKY AND BRENT HEATH

Midspring Tulips

Fosteriana

Fosteriana tulips were introduced in the early 1900s and bred to create the Darwin hybrids. With colors that range from bright red to orange, yellow, white, and also some bicolor blends, Fosteriana tulips perch on 10- to 20-inch stems, work well as bedding plants and in a mixed border, and perennialize easily. Sometimes called Emperor tulips, they are one of the first midseason tulips to bloom in spring. If you'd like tulips that have a good chance of returning year after year, Fosteriana cultivars are an excellent choice.

'Analita': short and sturdy, these tulips have a deep golden center that is surrounded by a ring of red extending to creamy white petals that age to pink as the flowers mature. Measuring only 12 to 14 inches, Analita looks delightful in the front of garden beds or along a walkway. Because the interior of the flower is so decorative, make sure to place it where it can be viewed up close and from above.

'Red Emperor' (also called 'Madame Lefeber'): this striking scarlet bloom is one of the most famous of the Fosteriana cultivars. With vivid red petals that open wide on sunny days to reveal a black center, it grows on sturdy 14- to 16-inch stems, tends to perennialize, and is likely to rebloom.

Analita

Red Emperor

Burning Heart

Darwin Hybrid

The Darwin tulip group might be considered the most popular tulips of our day—and with their large, cupped flowers and tall stems, you can see why. This midseason group comes from crossing the late-flowering Darwin tulips with *Tulipa fosteriana* , which have large flowers. Darwin hybrids also tend to be resilient in the garden, blooming for a few years without being lifted if their conditions are right.

'Apeldoorn': considered one of the best red tulips available, Apeldoorn is a scarlet stunner with a touch of black at the base. This classic Darwin hybrid often reblooms, with huge, 5-inch blooms on 22- to 24-inch stems.

'Pink Impression': with bright, rose-colored petals that appear warmer toward the center, turning pale at the edges, this candy-pink Darwin hybrid leaves an impression. Strong 20- to 24-inch stems make for an excellent cut flower and a good performer in the garden.

'Burning Heart': blooming yellow with bold red flames, this tulip fades to ivory as it ages, with a sunshine-colored center and striking black anthers. With huge blossoms on 18- to 22-inch stems, this award-winner makes an impact.

'Gudoshnik': each bloom is different, ranging from pale yellow petals delicately shot through with crimson, to deeper rich reds, golds, and orange. Floating on 24-inch stems, these flowers look entrancing when planted in drifts that will bloom in every color of the sunset. Gudoshnik is also available as a multi-petaled Double Late cultivar.

Calypso

Greigii

Blooming primarily in yellow, red, and white, Greigii tulips have an outer ring of petals that bend backward from the center as the flower opens. Hailing from Turkistan, they are midseason bloomers with fairly short stems (12 inches) and make excellent container plants. One striking feature is their variegated leaves, with stripes of magenta or purple, that add another decorative element and can be enjoyed long after the blooms have faded. Likely to perennialize, these tulips offer rewards for years to come.

'Fire of Love': with blazing red petals around a black center heart, these tulips feature unique blue-green leaves striped with purple, red, and a creamy yellow edge. A low grower (6- to 8-inch stems), this variety is limited in its availability, but always an eye-catcher.

'Calypso': a blaze of red-orange blooms with golden edges, this cultivar blooms on 6- to 12-inch stems with maroon stippling on the leaves. A bank of these flame-colored flowers will warm up your garden like nothing else.

'Quebec': this cream-colored tulip features a subtle striping of red brushed outward from a buttercup yellow center. With three to five flowers per bulb, these tulips give excellent value. They are a small (12-inch stems) but cheerful addition to the garden and excellent border plants with a long bloom period.

Triumph

One of the largest tulip groups, Triumph is sometimes also called Midseason. Arising from a cross between Single Early tulips with Darwin cultivars, Triumph features that classic wineglass shape and medium-tall stems (14 to 20 inches).

'Arabian Mystery': a stunner in maroon with a white edge, this cultivar attracts all the attention. This bicolored bloomer looks wonderful both in the garden or in the vase. This is a tulip to be planted in a special spot—when fully open, the white-tipped petals turn magenta and then fade white again at the base, with shades of lemon yellow; it's a showstopper.

'Pays Bas': a neutral, creamy white bloom, this tulip is excellent to set off other, more colorful cultivars. The fresh-looking flower perches on 18-inch stems, with a darker cream center on each petal that pales to white on the edges. An excellent choice to provide contrast with other flowers, or to plant against darker foliage where the blooms will look as if they are almost glowing.

'Flaming Flag': with large, ivory-colored blooms and a delicate striping of purple and lavender, this cultivar has an incandescent sheen to it. A real looker, this tulip is a springtime delight on 18- to 20-inch stems. An excellent cut flower. For a visual treat, plant in groups with white and purple Triumph tulips, such as Purple Flag.

Arabian Mystery and Pays Bas

Flaming Flag

We get so caught up weeding the yard that we completely miss the tulips that nature gives us for a few precious weeks. We postpone joy.

—AMIT SOOD

Mid to Late Spring Tulips

Parrot

As striking as a tropical bird, the Parrot group features tulips with colorful, contorted petals, often multicolored. Blooming in the mid to late season, these are some of the most striking tulips available—and while not all love them, they win a good number of hearts. Heights range, depending on cultivar, from 14 to 24 inches, and they always make a splash. It's said that the name refers to both the vivid "plumage" of the petals and the bud, which looks like the beak of a bird.

'Blumex': the colors and shapes of this tulip are reminiscent of modern art—with textures and tones that seem to melt together. In the garden or in the vase, these flowers deserve a closer look. With 20- to 22-inch stems, this is one of the latest tulips to bloom, and it certainly ends the season with a bang. Each flower is unique and utterly mesmerizing.

'Professor Rontgen': a tangerine dream, this is one of the largest parrot tulips, with fluted petals streaked in orange, yellow, cream, and green. Growing 18 to 24 inches, it looks like a Dutch master's painting when in the vase.

'Salmon Parrot': a striking salmon-orange tulip with touches of cream and stripes of green, the extravagant look of this tulip is a fan favorite with its ruffled sepals. A four-time award winner, the scalloped blooms perch on 20- to 22-inch stems.

Blumex

Salmon Parrot

Tulips are an incredibly diverse family of plants: Some have fringed petals, others have pointed ones, and some are so ruffled and full that they are commonly mistaken for peonies.

—ERIN BENZAKEIN

Rembrandt

The Rembrandt group originally consisted of tulips infected with the tulip breaking virus (TBV), which causes unique, feather-like streaks and coloration on tulip petals and resembles the sought-after blooms featured in the paintings of Rembrandt, among many others. At the time Rembrandt was painting, no one knew how or why a tulip "broke," and the effect was desired and much sought after. Tulip growers tried to cause tulips to break through various means, but no one could consistently and reliably reproduce the phenomenon.

It was Dorothy Cayley, a mycologist working in virus research at the John Innes Horticulture Institute in 1920s London, who proved that the broken look was the result of an infection being passed along by insects, most likely aphids. The seeds of the tulip were not affected, but the original tulip's bulb—and any bulbs that were produced from it—were. Over time, infected bulbs declined in vitality.

These days, TBV-infected tulips are no longer sold, although a few British enthusiasts continue to grow them (see page 113). The Rembrandt group features stable culti-vars that have been intentionally bred to exhibit the same coloration, though the color breaks on modern-day versions are a bit blockier. Rembrandt tulips come from different cul-tivar groups, so their heights and bloom times vary, but they all share the broken effect so desired in Rembrandt's day.

'Helmar' (Triumph tulip): Featuring maroon flames on a yellow base, Helmar makes for a striking combination with other dark cultivars such as Ronaldo. Growing on 22-inch stems, this is a statement tulip with historical pedigree, it looks equally at home in seventeenth-century Dutch paintings as it does in gardens today.

'Grand Perfection' (Triumph tulip): With vivid red flames that look like brushstrokes, Grand Perfection tulips start out with a creamy base color tinged slightly yellow, before fading to clean white. These 14- to 16-inch stems stand out in a garden bed or in a bouquet. Plant in blocks for greatest visual impact.

'Zurel' (Triumph tulip): With regal purple streaks on a base of white, Zurel is an eye-catcher, but the real show comes when the flowers open to reveal a golden center. With blooms that sway on 18- to 20-inch stems, Zurel will win fans, especially when planted en masse. This may be a tulip that speaks to history, but it also looks thoroughly modern and fresh.

Helmar (closed)

Helmar

Grand Perfection

Zurel

Viridiflora

The name Viridiflora refers to the green petal stripe (also called flame) this group has, reaching up from the stem. Like the Rembrandt tulips, this is another group based on a shared characteristic—the green coloring. These mid to late spring bloomers can last up to 3 weeks.

'China Town': looking like spring made manifest, this cultivar features ruffled pink petals streaked with green on 12-inch stems. With a creamy white edge on its leaves, this bloom looks beautiful in the garden or in a vase.

'Golden Artist': the pointed petals of deep, tawny gold and the distinctive green vein running up the outside of this bloom bring a warm glow to the garden. With slight ruffling to the petals and 14- to 16-inch stems, these tulips brighten any vase or flower bed.

'Esperanto': an eye-catching blaze of red and green, this cultivar attracts attention with its colorful blooms and silver-green foliage edged in white. A well-deserved award-winner, it grows on sturdy 10- to 12-inch stems and holds up well in a vase.

'Spring Green': another award-winning Viridiflora cultivar, this bloom feels like a breath of fresh air with its soft, green feathering on creamy white petals. With sturdy stems that grow 16 to 18 inches and flowers that open in sunlight to nearly 3 inches across, this tulip brings a bit of wildness to your flower beds and borders.

Esperanto

Cummins

Fringed

The unusual notched petal edge gives this group their name—fringed, like the edge of a shawl or carpet. Fringed cultivars originally occurred due to a mutation and come from different tulip groups. These mid to late spring bloomers bring a textural interest to bedding and container plantings. Because it's a small group and not widely planted, Fringed tulips always attract attention.

'Cummins': these lavender 4-inch blooms look like they've been frosted, with a crystalline white edge that is as unique as it is beautiful. These eye-catching blooms sway on 20-inch stems and look stunning, either planted en masse or scattered through the garden. Plant close enough to a pathway or patio to admire their unusual shape and coloring.

'Huis Ten Bosch': looking not unlike a cloud of cotton candy, these tulips feature a pale pink base that colors darker at the edges, ending in a delicate, jagged fringe. Sometimes called 'Candy Floss Tulips', these pink puffs are much stronger and more resilient than they appear. They look attractive on their own or planted with other fringed cultivars such as 'Cummins' or 'Daytona' (white).

'Swan Wings': with curving white petals and feathery serrated edges, Swan Wings is dramatic indeed. This cultivar's long, 22-inch stems are as graceful as a swan's neck, and the flowers have a delicate fragrance. In the garden or in a vase, these mid- to late-season bloomers are dazzling.

'Cuban Night': a stunning dark entry into the Fringed tulip group, the magenta-tinged petals of this variety add depth and drama to any tulip bed. An attractive pairing with pink, raspberry, or maroon cultivars, it adds a note of sophistication and mystery, swaying on 20- to 22-inch stems.

'Carousel': for those who want feathers *and* fringe, this tulip fits the bill, with raspberry streaks on a white background and sometimes hints of yellow. Growing on 18-inch stems, this bloom looks striking when grown alongside a dark cultivar, adding a cheerful whimsy.

'Queensland': stuffed with dark pink petals that lighten to a pale pink jagged edge, Queensland steals the show, either in a vase or in a garden bed. This unusual double fringed cultivar features large blooms up to 5 inches across that perch on 16- to 18-inch stems. Plant these stunners in a sheltered spot, so they won't be taken down by strong winds.

Cuban Night and Carousel

Fly Away

Lily-flowered

Some of the most elegant, visually appealing tulips hail from the Lily-flowered group, with elongated petals that taper to a sharp point. The group is not large, but they have been among the most beloved blooms in Turkey. Mid to late bloomers, these flowers arc outward on medium-height stems (10 to 24 inches), creating a sense of excitement and motion in the garden.

'Fly Away': a goblet-shaped flower in scarlet with golden edges, this cultivar looks like a flock of butterflies about to take flight as they sway on narrow 20-inch stems. Plant in a small mass for maximum impact; you won't regret it.

'Sarah Raven': named after the famed English gardener, writer, and tulip aficionado, this deep-magenta bloom looks elegant in the garden or in the vase. Flowering on 14- to 18-inch stems, this midseason bloomer lends a note of drama to flower arrangements or border plantings.

'Ballade': looking truly like a lily, this award-winner features purple-magenta petals edged in white. Opening to a star-shaped blossom with golden anthers on 22-inch stems, these dazzling flowers make an impact, especially when planted in drifts.

'Elegant Lady': muted and understated, these creamy flowers bloom with the slightest blush of pink and yellow on their curving petals, which fade to ivory with touches of violet. When the sun shines through these blooms, which perch on 20-inch stems, they light up with the most ethereal glow.

Late Season Tulips

Single Late

With egg-shaped flowers opening into cuplike blooms, Single Late group tulips have tall stems (18 to 30 inches) and flower late in the season. While often used in stunning border displays, the bulbs are not terribly vigorous.

'Antoinette': Starting out lemon yellow, these flowers blush pink at the edges, turning striped and then dark salmon-orange as they open. In addition to the changing color show, this tulip produces multiple blooms per stem, a bouquet effect in the garden on 18-inch stems.

'Menton': a delightful Easter egg in shades of rose pink with apricot edges, this bloom opens up to a coral-orange interior with a white center vein. Blooming longer than most cultivars, on 20- to 22-inch stems, it is an asset to any garden and deservedly popular (see page 142).

'Renown': this award-winning tulip features fuchsia-red oval blooms that pale toward the edge. This late bloomer perches on 24- to 26-inch stems—it reigns over the garden, and also stands up well in the vase.

'Violet Beauty': for the purple lovers out there, this lavender-blue cultivar will put on a show with petals that change color through the bloom period—sometimes edging more toward rose, sometimes more toward blue. It has a center blotch of ivory with dark anthers and blooms on 18-inch stems.

Antoinette

I didn't fully appreciate tulips
until a few years ago.
Once you stop trying to
control them,
their true beauty unfolds.

—JENNIFER PERILLO

Violet Beauty

Double Late (Peony)

Also called peony-flowered tulips, these double blooms feature rows of petals like petticoats. Mid to late bloomers, their heights vary by cultivar from 14 to 24 inches. Like the Double Early cultivars, even those who do not traditionally like tulips may fall in love with these generous blooms.

'Renown Unique': living up to its name, in peach with coral and touches of green, this cultivar sees the tulip season out with huge, fragrant flowers. Growing 20 inches high on sturdy stems, the unusual coloring—each bloom unique—makes an excellent cut flower for arrangements (see page 2).

'Carnival de Nice': looking very much like a tree peony when in full bloom, this is one of the last tulips to bloom each spring, but the wait is worth it for the red stripes on a white background and a party of petals. An award-winner, this striking flower blooms on 20-inch stems.

'La Belle Epoque': a cloud of dusky peach and cream, this double tulip is a puff of petals, growing pale as it ages. Perched on sturdy 12-inch stems, the unique, antique tones make this tulip a stunning cut flower.

'Black Hero': one of the dark tulip cultivars, this variety features a fluff of midnight-colored petals, almost like feathers, with a lustrous magenta sheen. An eye-catcher in the garden, it sways on 20- to 24-inch stems and wins admirers in any arrangement.

Carnival de Nice

La Belle Epoque

Black Hero

Turkestanica

Little Princess

Various Bloom Times

Species and Miscellaneous Group

This group includes the wild species varieties, sometimes called botanical tulips, and other varieties that don't fit elsewhere. Most of these tulips are small—4 to 10 inches—and naturalize more easily than modern hybrids. They are deer and rodent resistant, do not need to be deadheaded, and over time may grow into a durable ground cover. Plant these in the front of borders or in containers where they can be admired up close.

'Little Princess': with striking dark centers ringed in yellow and long, pointy orange-red petals, this tulip makes a big impact for such a small bloom. They grow only 4 to 8 inches, so make sure not to hide them away in the back of a garden bed. Flowers will open in full sun for a display of colorful stars.

'Turkestanica': with its creamy white petals, sun-colored center, and lavender-gray exterior, this beauty looks like a wildflower. These tiny wonders grow a bit taller than 'Little Princess' (8 to 12 inches) and look wonderful massed together. An extreme early bloomer—in some gardening zones they will bloom in March—each stalk produces several small, fragrant flowers (though some do not appreciate the scent).

'Lilac Wonder': these small tulips grow up to 8 inches tall and have tiny lavender petals surrounding a deep-yellow center. They have a high likelihood of perennializing. Plant in patches for greatest visual impact. Good for growing in warmer climates.

'Tarda': stars in the garden—with yellow centers and white tips—this variety has been grown by tulip aficionados since 1590. These award-winning blooms grow up to 6 inches and, when thickly planted, create a bank of thin, dark-green foliage set off with a constellation of starry blooms.

'Little Beauty': with hot pink/magenta petals that darken to a purple center with a rim of lavender, this small species tulip grows only 6 inches high, with narrow pale gray-green leaves. Similar to 'Little Princess', these tiny charmers open to full star shape in the sun and can produce multiple flowers from each bulb. Small but mighty, these fragrant blooms are worth seeking out (see page 10).

'Alba Coerulea Oculata': resembling Turkestanica, but featuring white star-like flowers with a steel blue heart, these early bloomers grow in mounds up to 6 inches tall. Excellent in rock gardens and long lived, these species tulips are small in size but big on charm (see page 10).

Lilac Wonder

Tarda

Tulip
Growing
& Flower
Culture

Deep in the drilled-in mud of
the fields behind me, our bulbs
are wrapped in their brittle
skins with their messages
of color stored inside. Blue
iris, yellow crocus, tulips of all
colors.

—ANNA SMAILL

Growing Tulips

Garden Design with Tulips

Tulips can be such dazzling, short-lived flowers that it's worth being thoughtful about how to incorporate them in your yard. There are a number of different approaches to planning a tulip garden.

Bedding Tulips—those stunning color displays of tulips in parks and public gardens rely on mass planting of bulbs in a well-defined space. These spaces can be large or small, but it's the densely planted bulbs that make for a knockout visual experience—either all in one color or a mixed palette. Once the bloom period is over, the bulbs will be replaced with other annuals for the next phase of the season. Bedding displays are usually planted with new bulbs each year and may not be the ideal approach for a backyard garden due to the labor and cost associated. But if you want to make a big color statement with tulips, this is the way to go.

Naturalized Tulips—for a more natural look, scatter bulbs throughout your landscape. Some gardeners actually advise tossing bulbs at random, for an effortless and unplanned effect—then dig and plant wherever they fall. You can plant these tulips bulbs in a field or meadow, or in a flower bed as well. The key is to plant in clumps and uneven numbers for an unaffected look. In flower beds, naturalized tulips can look stunning combined with forget-me-nots (*Myosotis sylvatica*), snowdrop anemone (*Anemonoides sylvestris*), creeping phlox (*Phlox stolonifera*), and more—but make sure to pick plants that are drought resistant, unless you plan on lifting your bulbs for the summer. The regular watering that many plants require to make it through the dry season is not recommended for tulip bulbs.

Mixed Bulb Beds—tulips look wonderful when paired with other bulbs, and this can be an easy way to create a continuous spring flower display. Crocuses and snowdrops are early spring, low-growing bulbs, but the season really kicks off with daffodils. There is a much wider variety of daffodils than most people realize, including multiflowered cultivars. They look beautiful interplanted with tulips—and, as daffodils are toxic and unappealing to most animals, they can discourage scavengers from bothering your tulips. Finally, hyacinths and Muscari (sometimes called grape hyacinth) round out the mid-height bulbs, adding both fragrance and blue, purple, and pink tones. As these bulbs all have different bloom times; by mixing them together you can have an ongoing floral display throughout early spring.

Border or Ribbon Planting—with their height, tulips make a stunning border when planted thickly along a walkway, hedge, or wall. Border plantings can be all one color, or a mix—just plant thickly for greatest visual impact (a narrow single row looks awkward and forced). Border plantings can also be made up of bulb mixtures as well. Keep in mind, however, that if you want to reuse tulip bulbs for the next spring, they must be left in place and their leaves allowed to wither naturally. Plan your border to accommodate this wilt period, or plan to replace the bulbs annually.

When to Plant

Tulips should be planted in the fall, when temperatures are 40 to 50 degrees F (4–10 degrees C). This means October or November, in the upper half of North America (Zones 4–8). In warmer climates (Zone 9 and above), that may be as late as December or even January. Zones 2 and 3 will want to plant as early as late September.

Planting tulip bulbs is not a task you should rush to get done early, however. By waiting until you've had a few overnight frosts, you may be able to avoid some of the viral and fungal diseases that infect tulips. Waiting can also help you dodge the worst of the foraging season, where squirrels and chipmunks may be tempted to dig up bulbs for their winter stores. You'll want to make sure not to wait until the ground freezes entirely, however. Tulip bulbs need to put out some roots before the soil freezes to be able to withstand the winter.

Because tulips need to experience a period of cold temperatures in order to bloom, if you are growing in a warmer climate (Zones 9 and 10), your bulbs will need to be intentionally chilled. You can purchase prechilled bulbs from growers that have been stored at least 12 weeks at 40 to 45 degrees F. You can also chill tulip bulbs yourself in a cool basement or in the refrigerator (they cannot be stored in the same refrigerator as ripening fruit, however, as many types of fruit produce ethylene gas and this will affect the viability of your bulbs). Bulbs that do not experience an adequate period of chill hours will not bloom.

Note that many growers and online bulb sources will sell out of favorite or sought-after tulip bulbs long before the planting season arrives, so it's best to not put off placing your order. Many sellers accept orders quite early and ship at the appropriate planting time, so there's no need to wait. Take note of what you want to plant during the spring bloom season, then submit your orders as soon as possible if there are particular bulbs you are interested in. Otherwise you may find your top choices have sold out for the season.

Where to Plant

Tulips like well-draining, sandy soil, either neutral or slightly acidic (pH of 6 to 6.5). Do not plant tulips in heavy clay or boggy soil, as the bulbs are likely to rot. Heavy soil can be lightened by digging in a significant amount of sand and organic material (in the Netherlands, tulips are often grown entirely in sand). When faced with boggy or clay conditions, it may be necessary to consider raised beds with soil that has been purchased, or to plant in other types of containers.

Like most bulbs, tulips are well suited for outdoor container growing. Pick cultivars with shorter, sturdy stems and plant deeply in the pots using potting soil (make sure the pots have drainage holes first). Single Early, Double Early, Kaufmanniana, and Greigii are all strong candidates for containers. Container-planted tulips will likely sprout and bloom slightly earlier than in-ground plantings, as pots warm up faster than flower beds.

Make sure to select a container large enough that the soil will provide adequate insulation and won't dry out too quickly. For potted tulips, plan for three bulbs per 4-inch pot, five bulbs per 6-inch pot, nine bulbs per 8-inch pot, and fifteen bulbs per 12-inch pot. Plant the bulbs with their flatter side facing out, toward the edge of the pot (this means the first leaves will grow outward and not crowd the middle). If you live in a climate with extended freezing temperatures, you may want to store smaller pots where they will be kept between 32 to 40 degrees F. An unheated basement or garage may work well.

In most climates, tulips want full day or afternoon sun. When growing in Zones 8 and above, half-day sunshine is adequate, as tulips do not like too much heat (flowers will last longer if shielded from hot or afternoon sunlight). When growing taller cultivars, make sure to select a site sheltered from strong spring winds that could damage long stems.

Preparing the Site

Loosen the soil in the area you would like to plant and amend with an inch of compost, working it into the soil. Tulips can either be planted in smaller bunches scattered among other plantings, or in a large swath for a more striking display. For smaller bunches, odd numbers of bulbs tend to look more natural than even numbers, and at least ten bulbs are needed for best visual impact. For larger plantings, plan for nine to twelve bulbs per square foot.

Planting Tulips

While tulip bulbs look squat and sturdy, they should be handled with care. The brown papery jacket should not be damaged or removed—though it may have cracked in transport. You may also see a bluish powdery substance on your bulbs, which is called transportation mold and can be wiped off, but any bulbs that are spongy or show rot or discoloration should be discarded. Make sure not to nick or otherwise damage the bulbs as you plant them.

Conventional wisdom has long advised that tulip bulbs should be planted two to three times as deep as the height of the bulb—generally, 3 to 6 inches. These days, however, advice has changed, as planting deeper—8 to 12 inches—yields various benefits. Deeper planting insulates the bulbs from soil temperature fluctuations and some diseases, it discourages scavenging animals, and it may promote blooms the following year. Deep planting also alleviates the need to stake taller cultivars. When deeply planted, taller tulips should be sturdy enough to withstand the weather.

Dig in a small handful of compost or well-aged manure into the native soil at the bottom of each of the holes—or, if you are planting a larger swath of flowers, it may be easier to dig a trench. Position each bulb, pointed end upward, about 3 inches apart, and backfill with the removed soil. Make sure to tamp down the soil completely when done, so there are no air pockets around the bulbs, and water well if you are not expecting rain in the following few days. The water is needed only once after planting to help activate growth. Unless you live in extremely dry conditions, winter weather should provide adequate moisture.

If you have a history of animals scavenging your tulip bulbs, you may want to be proactive with preventative measures. Squirrels like to dig up bulbs—and, while moles do not eat bulbs, voles and other rodents who use their underground tunnels do. These sorts of scavengers can be hard to ward off, but some gardeners have success by adding a layer of sharp gravel around the bulbs, as burrowing animals do not like to dig through anything prickly (dig a larger than needed hole, line with gravel, then fill with soil and tuck the bulb into the center). Other gardeners recommend adding pointy-edged holly leaves to the planting hole for the same effect (these will break down and compost over time, of course).

Those with intense burrowing pest issues could consider planting in trenches and lining the entire trench with chicken wire (chicken wire does rust over time, so you may be fishing small pieces of it out of your flower beds in decades to come). Professional flower growers sometimes use a plastic bulb crate, buried in this manner, to protect densely planted areas (the crates are lifted at the end of the season and the bulbs are not generally reused). There are also plastic "bulb baskets" made for this same purpose. Or to prevent scavengers from digging up newly planted bulbs, lay a bit of chicken wire or fine wire mesh (also called hardware cloth) on top of recent planting areas. The wire should be removed before spring growth gets underway.

Tulip Care

Tulips come with just about all the energy they need for the first year packed in their bulbs, so care is fairly simple. A little compost or aged manure dug in at planting time will support root and flower production, but otherwise tulips generally take care of themselves. The challenge is to keep them blooming. While some cultivars perennialize more easily than others, even rebloomers can fade out over time.

At issue is the way tulips reproduce. The mother bulb planted that first autumn will divide after it blooms in the spring and produce small bulblets or offshoots. These new, tiny bulbs do not have adequate energy stored to produce a flower yet, so it will take a few years to build up vigor.

To encourage reblooming, scatter a good flower fertilizer each spring when the tulip shoots begin to emerge (a fertilizer with a low nitrogen number, like 3-9-4, is recommended) and scratch it gently into the top layer of the soil with a gardening fork. Once the flowers have bloomed and faded, cut the main stalk back to the base to prevent the formation of seeds, but allow the leaves to remain intact and whither in their own time before removing—this helps build up energy for the next year. It can be helpful to add a layer of compost each autumn, both to enrich the soil and to provide some mulch and insulation for the bulbs. Planting the bulbs deeper than usual—8 to 12 inches—will also discourage bulb splitting.

There are some who recommend lifting tulip bulbs after they have bloomed in the spring and storing them through the dormant period before replanting in the fall as a way to encourage reblooming, especially in warmer climates (Zones 8–10), though other tulip experts think this is unnecessary. Not all cultivars are good candidates for lifting—Triumph, Fringed, Parrot, Double, and the Single groups (early and late) are best to experiment with lifting.

To do so, wait at least 3 weeks after the tulips have finished flowering (remove the spent flower stalk at the base, but not the leaves), then carefully dig up the bulbs with a garden fork. Any remaining dried leaves can be cut off, and bulbs should be washed gently to remove dirt, then laid in a single layer on a screen or plastic crate so they can dry completely. Label carefully before storing in a dark, cool, dry place with good ventilation and a stable temperature (65 to 68 degrees F is ideal). Make sure to check the bulbs monthly and remove any that show signs of rot or mildew. Replant in late autumn, adding compost to each bulb hole and top dressing with a fertilizer formulated for flowers.

If you are hoping for second- and even third-year blooms, certain tulip groups are more likely to be rebloomers. Cultivars from the Kaufmanniana, Fosteriana, and Greigii groups, and the species tulips, are good choices for reblooming and naturalizing.

Making the Most of Tulips

I always think you only
truly know a tulip if you've
lived with it and looked at
it on your kitchen table
for a week.

—SARAH RAVEN

Harvesting Tulips

How you harvest your tulips will influence how long they last in the vase. To maximize vase life, tulips should be picked when the bud has colored up on the outside but is still closed. By the time the flowers have opened, the petals are loose and will fall apart quickly. As with all flowers, it's best to pick them early in the morning, before the day has warmed. Avoid picking buds that have obvious damage or are stunted, as they may contain bacteria that will contaminate anything else in the vase.

Prior to harvesting, prepare by washing your intended receptacle. Any vase or bucket used should be washed with soap and hot water or cleaned with a mixture of nine parts water to one part bleach. The clippers or scissors you intend to use should be clean as well. Fill your bucket with luke-warm water to take with you when you go to harvest. Cut the tulips at the base of their stems and submerge immediately after cutting. Remove all foliage that would be under water in the vase. Because tulips tend to droop, wrap the bunch of flower stems firmly in newspaper or other sturdy paper (brown paper bags work well), so that all stems are straight and upright. Stand the tulips up in water for a few hours to fully hydrate them before arranging.

Recut the flowers once you're ready to arrange them. Submerge the stems under water and cut on a 45-degree angle. The slant maximizes the surface area able to absorb water and cutting underwater helps seal the cut.

Displaying Tulips

Tulips have such an effortless spring style, they hardly need any help at all. A simple bunch of single blooms looks fresh and uncontrived when placed in a glass jar. A more elaborate vase—and a more elaborate cultivar, like the multi-petaled blooms or Parrot varieties—triples the sophistication and impact with little effort. And tulips almost never look wrong—by just putting the stems in a vase and letting them fall where they may, you will likely come up with something natural and beautiful.

For more elaborate arrangements, support is needed for the soft tulip stems—especially for larger-headed cultivars, like Doubles, Parrots, and some of the Fringed group. When using a low bowl or other receptacle, flower grids are essential. These are usually made of wire and fit into the neck or opening of a vase or other arranging vessel. They can be purchased from floral supply shops or online sellers—or you can make your own with a small bit of chicken wire, bent to fill the space (use wire cutters to cut to size). It's also possible to make lovely organic-looking grids from lengths of wood or bamboo fastened in a cross pattern (use twine or flexible ties to secure the joints). Whatever you use, make sure to affix it to the vase or vessel (florist tape or sticky clay is helpful here).

Alternately, you can make a single-use grid by using tape—florist tape is ideal, but painter's tape or even clear tape should work in a pinch. Form a crisscross pattern across the neck of the receptacle that you will be using—just make sure to fill with water beforehand and dry the rim completely prior to applying tape or it will not stick properly. Once the grid is finished, insert the stems of your flowers and let the crisscross pattern help to hold them upright.

Another way to brace tulips or stabilize an arrangement is to incorporate branches for support, especially blooming branches that add another floral layer. Dogwood, forsythia, quince, pussy willow, viburnum, and plum blossom all are good candidates.

Tulips also mix well with other spring flowers such as hyacinths, lilac, and anemones. It's best to avoid mixing daffodils and tulips, however, as daffodils secrete a substance when cut that damages other flowers. (If you are determined, you can put the tulips and daffodils in separate vases of water for several hours, then combine the two in a clean vase along with a drop of bleach).

Tulips are also heliotropic—meaning the stems will grow and reach toward the sun—so however you arrange them, they will shift a bit over the days to come. Because of this it's good to rotate tulip arrangements a tiny bit each day so they don't grow unevenly and throw the arrangement off balance. Tulips are one of the only flowers that continue to grow after being cut—the stems will lengthen and the blooms will get bigger as they open. As a result, you may want to cut tulip stems slightly on the shorter side, otherwise you might have to do more trimming and maintenance along the way. But the pleasure of watching an arrangement of tulips stretch and unfurl is definitely worth it.

Forcing Tulips

Tulips, like a number of other bulbs, are excellent flowers for forcing—planting in pots to be grown inside in the middle of winter. While forcing does require planning and effort, the result is rewarding. There is nothing so cheerful as a pot of spring blooms to brighten up a dull, gray day.

Select your bulbs carefully. The best tulips for forcing are Double Early, Single Early, Triumph, or one of the species cultivars. Make sure the bulbs used are firm and without blemish. It's generally recommended to use all the same cultivar in one pot to assure uniform growth, though it can be stunning to mix tulips with daffodils and hyacinths. It's best to pick tulips that are on the shorter side so support is not necessary.

The fun of forcing tulips is that you can use untraditional planting containers—a rustic wooden box, an old enamel colander (line with moss before adding soil), or a large glass apothecary jar. While it's best if the container has drainage holes, it is possible to add gravel to a nondraining pot or jar and use that to keep the bulbs above water level (the roots may eventually rot in the water, but not usually until after the bulb has bloomed).

There are a few different ways to force tulips. The easiest is to use prechilled bulbs, which should be planted as soon as you can after purchase. If it is not possible to plant immediately, store the bulbs at 40 to 45 degrees F (4 to 7 degrees C) until you are ready to pot them. If prechilled bulbs are stored at room temperature for too long, they will lose all benefit of the chilling treatment and you will need to start the process over again and chill them yourself.

To chill bulbs yourself, store them in a cool, temperature-stable basement or garage that is consistently 40 to 45 degrees F (4 to 7 degrees C) for at least 12 weeks. You can also store them in a refrigerator if the bulbs are kept dry and no fruit is stored there (the ethylene gas that fruit emits as it ripens will damage the tulip bulbs).

Once chilled for 3 months, you can either place the bulbs in a pot filled with sterile potting mix or in a container filled with gravel (nestle the bulbs into the gravel and fill with water to just below the base of the bulbs; if the bulb is submerged, it will rot). Keep the bulbs in a cool and preferably dark location for several days, then gradually increase the temperature and bring them into the light. The roots should grow down into the gravel and wick the water up to the bulb.

A more traditional method of forcing is to pot the bulbs in potting soil (make sure the pointy tips of the bulbs are poking out above the soil line) and then chill the pot and bulbs together for at least 12 weeks. Select a pot or vessel with drainage holes and fill with sterile potting mix. The full pot can be stored in the refrigerator, in a cool basement, or even buried outside in a woodchip pile, depending on your climate (bury deeply to allow the woodchips to insulate the pot from freezing temperatures). It should have some covering on it to make sure light is not getting in (newspaper or mulch should do the trick).

Once you remove the pot from the chilling area, uncover the bulbs and move them initially to a dark, cool spot, then within a few days to a warmer spot with light. Monitor the moisture level of the bulbs and keep the soil slightly moist but never soggy. Once the bulbs have started growing, rotate the pot or container every few days so the tulips grow straight upward. It will take about a month after the bulbs have begun to grow before you can expect blooms.

Edible Petals

Tulip bulbs are edible—indeed, they are a member of the same family as onion—but it's debatable how enjoyable they are to eat (see page 20). The petals, however, are another story.

The wide color variety of tulip petals lend themselves to a great many decorative uses. Make sure to use only garden-grown flowers—or from a trusted source that grows organically—as commercial plants may have been treated with sprays or chemicals. Petals will last 1 or 2 days after being removed from the flower heads, but it's best to store them in the refrigerator until you are ready to use them.

Here are some favorite ways to incorporate edible petals into your meals and parties:

Top salads with tulip petals for a bit of whimsey and color. Make sure to sprinkle on the salad *after* it has been dressed, as salad dressing will weigh down the petals and make them stick to the bowl.

Tulips can make a beautiful decoration for frosted cakes or cupcakes—either scattered at random, or intentionally applied according to a design for a more elaborate, artistic display. Apply petals no more than a few hours before serving.

Freeze petals into ice cubes to be used for party drinks—either for the drinks themselves, or to fancy up a bucket for wine or champagne (just be prepared to refresh with new ice to keep it looking festive as the event goes on).

Use tulips to liven up a cheese plate. The larger, cuplike petals (Single Early or Late cultivars) are strong enough to handle a bit of spreadable cheese with a sprinkle of fresh herbs at their base for a unique botanical snack.

Flower Viewing

I love tulips better than any
other spring flower; they
are the embodiment of alert
cheerfulness and tidy grace.

—ELIZABETH VON ARNIM

Istanbul Tulip Festival

ISTANBUL, TURKEY

The Dutch may be known for their tulips, but the Turks got there first—and the Istanbul Tulip Festival celebrates this fact. Thirty million tulip bulbs are planted throughout city parks, along the streets, and in roundabouts, transforming public spaces into a carpet of color and design throughout April. One of the hubs of the festival is Emirgan Park, where a series of villas host art demonstrations—glassblowing, paper marbling, calligraphy, painting—and musical performances are offered throughout the park. In front of Sultanahmet Camii (also known as the Blue Mosque), a display of half a million tulips arranged in the form of the largest flower carpet in the world replicates symbols used by traditional Turkish carpetmakers and is laid out in a different design each year. Local residents join in the celebration by planting tulips on their balconies and in window boxes. This explosion of color, especially as the city wakes from winter, is a fitting tribute to the site that introduced tulips to the Western world.

Keukenhof (the Garden of Europe)

LISSE, NETHERLANDS

Partway between Amsterdam and Leiden, Keukenhof is perhaps the best-known flower garden in the world. Laid out over nearly 80 acres on the former hunting grounds of a fifteenth-century castle, Keukenhof is named after the kitchen herb and vegetable garden. The gardens were originally planned in 1857 by designers Jan David Zocher and his son Louis Paul Zocher (the duo also designed Amsterdam's Vondelpark). Modern-day Keukenhof was established in 1949 by a consortium of bulb growers and flower exporters as a way to display their products. Each year's floral display includes 7 million flower bulbs—tulips, daffodils, hyacinths, irises, and more. The displays are designed for longevity, with three bulbs planted in each spot. Once the most shallowly positioned bulb blooms, it is cut back to make room for the next, so the displays are able to last the full 8-week display period. Keukenhof is open to the public for the spring bloom period, from mid-March to mid-May.

Keukenhof.nl

Hortus Bulborum

LIMMEN, NETHERLANDS

North of Amsterdam, in the town of Limmen, lies a small but significant tulip garden. It was established in the 1920s by avid gardener Pieter Boschman, who realized that many of the older tulip varieties were no longer being offered by commercial tulip growers. Fearing these varieties might be lost forever, Boschman began gathering and planting them on land next to the school where he was headmaster. Over nearly 100 years, the garden has grown to 4 acres and encompasses a collection of more than 2,500 tulips. Visitors are able to see tulips such as 'Duc van Tol Red and Yellow', which dates back to 1595. The red-and-white streaked 'Zomerschoon' is a broken tulip first registered in 1620 that commanded high prices in the tulip mania of the 1600s, while *Tulipa acuminata*, with unusually long and needle-like petals, is beloved by Turkish growers. Run entirely by volunteers, each spring this botanical museum is transformed into a carefully labeled patchwork quilt of color and texture, anchored by the old stone church of Limmen. It's a stunning sight.

Hortus-Bulborum.nl

ENGLISH FLORIST TULIPS

In the United Kingdom, a piece of tulip history lives on—in the Wakefield and North of England Tulip Society. Founded in 1836, it was one of numerous societies that championed "florist tulips," those flamboyant blooms that are "broken" due to a bulb disease (*florist* was an early term for flower enthusiast). Broken tulips were wildly popular and sought after by the Dutch in the 1600s, but they found a fond and enduring home among the craftspeople and working class of northern England, who raised them to breed and show. These shows were not fancy events—they took place in pubs, and the tulips were displayed in brown beer bottles.

Within florist tulips, there are different types of bulbs and classifications. "Bizarre" refers to a base yellow tulip overlaid with a darker color pattern; "Rose" is a white bloom with red or pink coloration; and "Bybloemen" is white with black or purple. When speaking of the color patterns, "feathered" refers to colors that emerge from the petal edge, while "flame" is used to describe color that runs up the middle from base to petal tip. To see a roomful of these striking blooms is quite a sight.

The Wakefield group is the only society that remains from this period of tulip fancying. Each May sees an annual show that features dozens of these vintage cultivars, still displayed in brown beer bottles, bred and preserved by loyal members for nearly 200 years.

TulipSociety.co.uk

Great Dixter

NORTHIAM, EAST SUSSEX, UK

Family home of gardener and writer Christopher Lloyd (1921–2006), Great Dixter is the East Sussex Arts and Crafts–style garden and nursery that was his life's work and continues to draw visitors from around the world to study and appreciate the informal but highly visual succession planting that Lloyd employed. While the gardens are beautiful year-round, in springtime they showcase a unique and integrated approach to tulips and other bulbs. Rather than using the blooms as blocks or large swaths of color, Great Dixter head gardener Fergus Garrett and his team thread them through other plantings with a deliberate and judicious hand, playing off the surrounding foliage so they are shown to best advantage. Once the bulbs have bloomed, the surrounding perennials grow up around them and hide the withering tulip leaves. Garrett trials different tulip cultivars to find those that are likely to repeat bloom; the large pots of thickly planted bulbs on display each year may well be testing their potential for future plantings. Great Dixter showcases the beauty of the flowers in an exuberant, mixed spring landscape.

GreatDixter.co.uk

Grand Perfection

Ottawa Tulip Festival

OTTAWA, CANADA

The roots of the Ottawa Tulip Festival go back to World War II, when German Nazi forces invaded the Netherlands and the Dutch royal family fled the country. Queen Wilhelmina set up a government in exile in Great Britain, while her daughter and heir, Princess Juliana, took refuge in Canada. The princess gave birth to her third child, Princess Margriet, while in Ottawa in 1943—and the Canadian government granted extraterritorial status to her hospital room, making it a temporary Dutch possession so the baby would be considered a full Dutch citizen. In honor of the hospitality she received, and the role Canadian troops played in liberating the Netherlands, once the war was over Princess Juliana sent a gift of 100,000 tulip bulbs, with the promise of more each year for her lifetime. These days the Canadian Tulip Festival is centered at Commissioners Park, on the shores of Dow's Lake, and celebrates the tulip as an international symbol of peace and friendship.

TulipFestival.net

Holland Ridge Farms

CREAM RIDGE, NEW JERSEY

East Coasters looking to get their tulip fix can head to 60 acres of u-pick flowers at Holland Ridge Farms to enjoy the blooms and the opportunity to cut your own bouquet. Holland Ridge is the dream of Casey Jansen Sr., who immigrated from the Netherlands as a teenager, bringing with him knowledge passed down by generations of his bulb growing family. Casey founded the Holland Greenhouses company, which sells flowers up and down the East Coast, but the whole Jansen family pitches in for the u-pick season—planting more than 1 million bulbs. The results are fields of stunning colors and shapes, filled with families and friends out to enjoy a spring day. There are food trucks to provide lunch, baked goods available in the barn, and picnic tables throughout the farm. A tractor offers free hayrides; and there are farm animals to visit, a small museum on Dutch tulip planting, and pony rides and a petting zoo on weekends. Partway between New York and Philadelphia, Holland Ridge's u-pick season begins mid-April and runs for 2 to 3 weeks.

HollandRidgeFarms.com

Tulip Time Festival

HOLLAND, MICHIGAN

Established by Dutch immigrants, the town of Holland, Michigan, is now home to the largest tulip festival in the United States. Held each year on the first full week of May, the festival traces its roots to a biology teacher who suggested planting tulips as a community beautification project. In 1928 the city council approved her idea and began planting 100,000 Dutch tulip bulbs. These days the festival includes 4.5 million bulbs, three parades, a Dutch market, craft fair, and a celebration of cultural traditions such as costumed *klompen* (wooden clog) dancing. There are even fireworks and a Tulipalooza concert. The town holds tight to its Dutch and settler history, featuring several museums and historical homes, a Dutch Village theme park and wooden shoe factory, and a garden with a working windmill that grinds flour. Part flower festival, part living museum, Tulip Time is now approaching its hundredth year of celebrating the tulip and the country that adopted it.

TulipTime.com

Skagit Valley Tulip Festival

SKAGIT VALLEY, WASHINGTON

Each April the farmland north of Seattle is striped with brilliant colors of red, yellow, purple, and pink as the tulip fields of Washington's Skagit Valley come into bloom. The area's tulip history began in the late 1800s, when an English immigrant was struck by how well the tulip bulbs he planted multiplied, and he reached out to Dutch growers for advice. When he sent them samples, a group of growers came to see "this land which could grow bulbs equal to Holland." The US Department of Agriculture began tulip trials shortly after, and the Washington bulb industry—now worth $12 million annually—was born. The festival runs for an entire month, with flower fields, display gardens, a gala, an organized cycling event, and a nightly salmon barbeque. While the two display gardens—Tulip Town and RoozenGaarde—require admittance tickets, the growing fields are scattered through-out the valley (locations change every year due to crop rotation) and can be viewed at any time.

TulipFestival.org

Wooden Shoe Tulip Festival

WOODBURN, OREGON

The Iverson family of Oregon began growing tulips in 1974, but it was in 1985 that they opened their fields to the public for Easter weekend—and Wooden Shoe Tulip Fest was born. Now celebrated from mid-March to the beginning of May, the festival features 40 acres of tulips in bloom, a display garden, tram and hayrides around the fields, a children's play area, a craft market, weekend hot-air balloon rides over the blooming fields, and a 5– and 10–kilometer fun run and half marathon. There are even special access tickets for photographers looking to capture the fields at sunrise. And because they are located in the wine region of Oregon's Willamette Valley, the youngest generation of the family added grape vines in 2009 and now runs Wooden Shoe Vineyards. Sipping sparkling Albariño while touring the fields on one of their Wine Wagon Tours is a peak spring experience.

WoodenShoe.com

OTHER TULIP FESTIVALS OF NOTE

Tulip Time Festival, Pella, Iowa
visitpella.com/tulip-time-faq/

Chilliwack Tulip Festival, Fraser Valley, British Columbia, Canada
chilliwacktulipfest.com

Tulip Festival at Thanksgiving Point, Lehi, Utah
thanksgivingpoint.org/events/tulip-festival/

Albany Tulip Festival, Albany, New York
albany.org/things-to-do/events-calendar/annual-events-and-festivals/the-albany-tulip-festival/

Festival of Spring, Nokesville, Virginia
burnsidefarms.com/spring

Richardson Farm Tulip Festival, Spring Grove, Illinois
richardsonadventurefarm.com/TulipFestival/Home

Spring Bloomfest, Stevens-Coolidge House, North Andover, Massachusetts
thetrustees.org/program /springbloomfest-at-stevens-coolidge-house-gardens/

Tonami Tulip Park

TOYAMA, JAPAN

On the western coast of Japan lies the town of Tonami, the center of tulip cultivation in Japan starting in 1918. Today the town hosts a 2-week festival to celebrate the flowers at bloom time, featuring 2.5 million bulbs in flower fields, landscaped gardens, and a variety of innovative displays. There is a Tulip Aroma Garden, which showcases the different tulip fragrances, walls of blooms in the Valley of Flowers, a lake with floating islands of tulips, and a Gallery of Tulips that displays all the blooms in a glass capsule. There is even a Tulip Tower you can climb for an aerial view of the park and flower beds, and live stage performances—including a flower fashion show. The festival runs from mid-April to early May, but the tulip park is open year-round, as the indoor displays can be filled with bulbs that have been forced even off-season.

Fair.TulipFair.or.jp

Flair

Glossary

ANTHER: the end portion of a flower stamen that produces pollen.

BASAL PLATE: the compressed stem or base of a bulb that connects to the roots and scales.

BROKEN TULIP: a tulip infected with the tulip breaking virus (see page 134), or one whose petals exhibit the two-color effect that mimics the virus.

BULB: a rounded, underground storage organ present in some plants—notably tulips, lilies, and onions—that goes dormant in warm, dry weather.

CULTIVAR: a cultivated species of a plant intentionally created through breeding.

DOUBLE: a tulip form featuring two rows of petals and divided in two groups—Double Early tulips and Double Late tulips.

FEATHERED: an effect seen with tulip breaking virus where two colors separate; feathered tulips have no central petal flame and feature fine, thin striping of both colors.

FILAMENT: the male portion of a flower's reproductive system, the filament holds the anther; together they make up the stamen.

FLAME: a streak of color on a tulip petal that begins at the center of the petal base and goes upward.

HYBRID: a plant cultivar created by crossing two parent plants to pass on specific desirable traits.

INNER SCALES: scales are the layers of a tulip, onion, or lily bulb; inner scales are closer to the bud stalk.

OVARY: part of the female organ of a flower, it consists of the enlarged basal portion of the pistil.

PARROT TULIP: a tulip group that features scalloped, textured petals, first introduced in 1630.

PISTIL: the female organs of a flower, includes the stigma, style, and ovary.

SCALES: fleshy leaves or layers of a bulb that surround the bud stalk and provide nourishment.

SEPALS: an outer part of the flower bud, usually green, that surrounds and protects the flower while in bud form.

SPECIES: the original or wild form of a plant or flower.

SPORT: a naturally occurring mutation off a standard flower or plant; desirable sports will be cultivated and given a name.

STAMEN: the male reproductive portion of a plant, located in the center of the flower; made up of the anther (upper, pollen-bearing portion) and the filament (stem on which the anther rests).

STYLE: part of the female organs of a plant; a slender stalk that connects the ovary and stigma.

TEPALS: used to describe petals and sepals when there is little discernable difference between the two (i.e. with tulips and lilies).

TUNIC: brown, papery skin that surrounds and protects a bulb.

TULIP BREAKING VIRUS (TBV): a virus that causes tulip colors to become unstable and "break." See more on pages 56 and 134.

VARIETY: naturally occurring plant or flower that grows true to form; not an intentionally cultivated or hybridized version.

Pests & Diseases

APHIDS: tiny insects—less than a ¼ inch—that suck the nutrients out of plants, aphids multiply quickly, looking like a gray-green crust. Sometimes they appear white, black, brown, green, yellow, or gray. Aphids like the juicy new plant growth and will generally hide on the undersides of leaves. Small aphid infestations may be remedied with a blast of water from a hose several times a week, or by hand picking (make sure to destroy removed leaves, which harbor aphid eggs). Or try spraying plants with a solution of water and a few drops of dish soap. For more persistent infections, applications of insecticidal soap and horticultural oils have both proven successful.

BASAL ROT: brown spots, or white/pink mold on the bulbs may indicate basal rot, a fungus (*Fusarium oxysporum f. sp. tulipae*) that harbors in the soil and plant material. Basal rot generally occurs in storage. If planted, the bulb may grow, but the leaves are likely to be deformed, stunted, or yellow, the stem may be streaked with brown, and the plant will generally die. Make sure to inspect any new bulbs before planting, to assure they are not infected. Make sure to plant your bulbs in soil that drains well, and avoid piercing the bulb on planting. If basal rot is suspected in planted tulips, remove immediately, along with the surrounding soil, and dispose of (not in a home composting system). Avoid replanting tulips in the same spot the next year.

BOTRYTIS (GRAY MOLD): a common disease found in the garden, especially among fruit and flowers. The fungus appears as water-soaked areas, which will change to brown, orange, reddish, or fuzzy gray and cause the leaves and flower to wilt. *Botrytis cinerea* infects plants that have been weakened or damaged in some way and grows in damp environments, so water your tulips in the morning when the plants will have a full day to dry out, and also avoid overhead watering. Plant with adequate spacing for airflow and remove withered leaves and spent blossoms to discourage any disease growth. Make sure to clean your clippers between pruning different plants, so as not to pass along any disease.

MITES: bulb mites are small, white arachnids with reddish-brown legs that live in the surrounding soil and feed on the bulbs. They enter the bulb where the surface has been pierced or damaged by rot, then continue to degrade the bulb by eating away at it. Prevent mites by inspecting all bulbs before planting them (discard any that have damage—not in a composting system)—and making sure your soil drains well, as overly moist soil is to be avoided. Spider mites are a different pest, which are tiny and attack stems, leaves, and flower heads, sucking the moisture out of them and leaving a white or yellow speckled pattern behind. Test for spider mites by shaking your tulip over a sheet of white paper to see if you can dislodge the tiny arachnids. You can treat spider mites like aphids and spray them off with water or insecticidal soap.

NEMATODES: stem and bulb nematodes are tiny, wormlike animals that feed on soft plant tissue, which results in distorted growth and cell death. Nematodes can be difficult to diagnose, as the worms can only be seen with a microscope. Noticeable symptoms include stunted, yellowish foliage with small, yellow speckles on the underside of the leaves. Bulbs, when dug up, may be soft and/or rotten. While there are no pesticides available to the home gardener for stem and bulb nematodes, infestations can be prevented through good sanitation practices—make sure to purchase good quality bulbs from reliable nurseries. If an infestation is suspected, remove the bulbs, foliage, and soil surrounding the plant and dispose of diseased material (not in a home composting system).

SLUGS AND SNAILS: slugs and snails prefer damp environments, so make sure your tulips have good drainage and be careful using mulch or other materials that will create inviting habitat. If you find that the local slug and snail population is still damaging your tulips, laying down a snail and slug bait should protect your flowers. Make sure to select a brand that is safe for pets, children, and wildlife. Finally, nightly inspections can help you find and dispose of these hungry pests.

TULIP BREAKING VIRUS (TBV): affecting only pink, purple, and red tulips, TBV causes a feather-like pattern on the tulip petals in white or a darker color. While the patterning can be striking, the virus weakens the bulb and can be spread to other tulips by aphids or greenfly, so it is best to remove and destroy any infected bulbs (though you can cut the flowers and bring them inside to enjoy in a vase).

TULIP CROWN ROT: caused by the fungus *Sclerotium delphinii*, which will turn leaves red as the tulips wilt and die. The bulb may be covered by a white coating of mycelium, and there may be brown spots on the stem. If found, remove infected bulbs and the surrounding soil and dispose of (not in a home composting system).

TULIP FIRE: caused by the fungus *Botrytis tulipae*, which can grow in damp and wet environments, tulip fire first appears as spots on the leaves and flowers, which then can become twisted and deformed. This may be followed by a gray mold, and the flowers or leaves may rot. To prevent tulip fire, plant in well-draining areas with good airflow. If signs of disease appear, quickly remove any infected bulbs and their attached foliage and dispose of (not in a home composting system). Avoid planting tulips in that area for 3 years.

WILDLIFE (SQUIRRELS, MICE, VOLES, ETC.): tulip bulbs are attractive to a wide number of animals. Squirrels will dig up tulip bulbs to eat or store, while voles and mice will use underground tunnels and gnaw out the bulbs while under the soil. Because tulips are planted in the early autumn, prime foraging season for squirrels, they are particular targets. If your climate is warm enough, consider delaying your planting to late October or November. Underground pests can be discouraged by adding crushed gravel or crushed oyster shells in a band around the planting area or planting hole, as voles—and moles, whose tunnels voles often use—do not like digging through abrasive materials. You can also set traps for voles and mice or use repellants in the form of predator urine (fox or coyote, which can be purchased), but such repellants need to be reapplied and may not be effective underground. Finally, if pest pressure is just too high, consider making a cage that will be buried to enclose the planted bulbs and allow the tulips to sprout through the openings (chicken wire is useful for this, but will rust and break over time). You can also try interplanting your tulips with daffodils, which are unappealing to wildlife and may ward them off.

WIREWORMS: about ¾ of an inch long, wireworms are the larval stage of the click beetle (named because it makes a clicking sound when it flips over). The beetles are found in the soil, where they will burrow into bulbs and hollow out the stems, killing the tulip. Because the larvae live under-ground, they are hard to locate, but easy to identify when found during springtime weeding. Make sure to destroy any wireworms you find.

Couleur Cardinal

Resources

The more you discover about tulips, the more you may enjoy them. Tulip mania can strike even today, and you might find yourself becoming fascinated with the history, variety, and beauty of these bulbs. Here are some resources to help you learn more about spring's most colorful flower.

Associations, Museums, & General Resources

The KAVB

The Royal General Bulb Growers' Association (*De Koninklijke Algemeene Vereeniging voor Bloembollencultuur*, or KAVB) was established in 1860 to coordinate floral exhibitions. It has since expanded to take on all issues surrounding the tulip bulb industry. For those outside the industry, one important role the KAVB plays is to host a tulip registry that tracks name, date of registration, description, and hybridizer. The registry is accessible on their website (English version available) and is searchable by nonmembers.

Kavb.nl/english

Amsterdam Tulip Museum

In the charming neighborhood of Jordaan, along the canal on Prinsengracht, is the Amsterdam Tulip Museum. This small but significant museum traces the history of the tulip from its origins in the Central Asian highlands to Turkey during the Ottoman Empire, through Dutch tulip mania, to the modern-day industry of growing, breeding, and selling bulbs worldwide. The museum provides insight into how integral the tulip has been to Dutch life.

Prinsengracht 116 | 1015 EA Amsterdam, Netherlands
AmsterdamTulipMuseum.com

Museum de Zwarte Tulip (Black Tulip Museum)

A 10-minute walk from the gardens of Keukenhof, in the town of Lisse, lies the Black Tulip Museum, an interactive exhibition that covers 500 years of history of the bulb-growing region and the new, science-fueled developments of today's bulb industry. Additionally, tulips are featured as the inspiration for the art they've always been—in paintings, and on glass, silver, and china. The museum is housed in a converted bulb shed, and in the spring, tulips bloom in the museum garden. There is also a café that serves refreshments.

Heereweg 219 | 2161 BG Lisse, Netherlands
MuseumdeZwarteTulp.nl/

Tulip Suppliers

Breck's Bulbs
PO Box 65
Guilford, IN 47022-0065
Brecks.com

Brent and Becky's Bulbs
7463 Heath Trail
Gloucester County, VA
23061
BrentandBeckysBulbs.com

John Scheepers
23 Tulip Drive
Bantam, CT 06750
JohnScheepers.com

Old House Gardens
4175 Whitmore Lake Road
Ann Arbor, MI 48105
OldHouseGardens.com

RoozenGaarde
(Washington Bulb Company)
16031 Beaver Marsh Road
Mount Vernon, WA 98273
Tulips.com

Terra Ceia Farms
3810 Terra Ceia Road
Pantego, NC 27860
TerraCeiaFarms.com

K. van Bourgondien
PO Box 1000
Babylon, NY 11702
DutchBulbs.com

White Flower Farm
167 Litchfield Road (Route 63)
Morris, CT 06763
WhiteFlowerFarm.com

Wooden Shoe Tulip Farm
33814 South Meridian Road
Woodburn, OR 97071
WoodenShoe.com

Further Reading

Tulips: Beautiful Varieties for Home and Garden, by Jane Eastoe (Gibbs Smith, 2019).

Tulips: For North American Gardens, by Becky and Brent Heath (Bright Sky Press, 2001).

The Tulip: The Story of the Flower That Has Made Men Mad, by Anna Pavord (Bloomsbury Publishing, 2019).

The Plant Lover's Guide to Tulips, by Richard Wilford (Timber Press, 2015).

Montreux

Menton

TARA AUSTEN WEAVER is an award-winning writer, editor, and avid gardener. She is the author of several books, including *Orchard House*, a finalist for the 2016 Washington State Book Awards, *Growing Berries and Fruit Trees in the Pacific Northwest*, and the Little Book of Flowers series: *Peonies* and *Dahlias*. She is trained as a Permaculture Designer, Master Gardener, and Master Composter/Soil Builder. Tara writes frequently about gardening, agriculture, food, art, travel, and social justice. More information can be found on taraweaver.com.

EMILY POOLE was born and raised in the mountain town of Jackson Hole, Wyoming. After receiving her BFA in illustration from the Rhode Island School of Design, she returned west to put down roots in the mossy hills of Oregon. She can be found exploring tidepools and cliffsides, gathering inspiration, and making artwork about our fellow species and how to be better neighbors with them.

Printed in China

SASQUATCH BOOKS with colophon is a registered trademark
of Penguin Random House LLC

27 26 25 24 23 22   9 8 7 6 5 4 3 2 1

Illustrations: Emily Poole | Editor: Hannah Elnan
Production editor: Peggy Gannon | Designer: Anna Goldstein

Library of Congress Cataloging-in-Publication Data
Names: Weaver, Tara Austen, author.
Title: Tulips : a little book of flowers / Tara Austen Weaver;
illustrations by Emily Poole.
Description: Seattle, WA : Sasquatch Books, [2023]
Identifiers: LCCN 2022005763 | ISBN 9781632174444 (hardcover)
Subjects: LCSH: Tulips. | Field guides.
Classification: LCC SB413.T9 W43 2023 | DDC 635.9/3469–dc23/
eng/20220218
LC record available at https://lccn.loc.gov/2022005763

Grateful acknowledgment is made to the following:
Page 13: Reproduced by permission from Tom Lodewijk,
The Book of Tulips (New York: The Viking Press, 1979)

ISBN: 978-1-63217-444-4
Sasquatch Books
1325 Fourth Avenue, Suite 1025
Seattle, WA 98101

SasquatchBooks.com

FSC

MIX
Paper | Supporting
responsible forestry
FSC® C008047
www.fsc.org